WHAT ON EARTH IS AN
ECHIDNA

JENNY TESAR

 A BLACKBIRCH PRESS BOOK

WOODBRIDGE, CONNECTICUT

Published by Blackbirch Press, Inc.
One Bradley Road, Suite 104
Woodbridge, CT 06525

Printed in the United States

10 9 8 7 6 5 4 3 2 1

Photo Credits:
Cover, title page: ©Kathie Atkinson/Oxford Scientific Films/Animals Animals.
Pages 4—5: ©C. Allan Morgan/Peter Arnold, Inc.; page 6: ©Tom McHugh/Photo Researchers, Inc.; page 9: ©Roland Seitre/Peter Arnold, Inc.; page 11 (top): ©A. B. Joyce/Photo Researchers, Inc.; page 11 (middle): ©Roland Seitre/Peter Arnold, Inc.; page 11 (bottom): ©Hans & Judy Beste/Animals Animals; page 12 (top): ©Hans & Judy Beste/Animals Animals; page 12 (bottom): ©Gerard Lacz/Animals Animals; page 13: ©C. Allan Morgan/Peter Arnold, Inc.; page 14: ©Kathie Atkinson/Oxford Scientific Films/Animals Animals; page 15: ©Hans & Judy Beste/Animals Animals; page 16: ©David C. Fritts/Animals Animals; page 17: ©John Eastcott/Yva Momatiur/Animals Animals; page 19: ©H. Reinhard/Okapia/Photo Researchers, Inc.; pages 20—21: ©Bill Bachman/Photo Researchers, Inc.; page 20 (inset): ©Kathie Atkinson/Oxford Scientific Films/Animals Animals; pages 22—23: ©C. Allan Morgan/Peter Arnold, Inc.; pages 24—25: ©C. Allan Morgan/Peter Arnold, Inc.; page 26: ©Kathie Atkinson/Oxford Scientific Films/Animals Animals; page 27: ©Hans & Judy Beste/Animals Animals; page 28: ©Roger Archibald/Animals Animals.
Map by Blackbirch Graphics, Inc.

Library of Congress Cataloging-in-Publication Data
Tesar, Jenny E.
What on earth is an echidna? / by Jenny Tesar. — 1st ed.
  p.   cm. — (What on earth series)
  Includes bibliographical references and index.
  ISBN 1-56711-098-3 (lib. bdg.)
  1. Tachyglossidae—Juvenile literature. [1. Echidnas. 2. Monotremes.]
I. Title. II. Series.
QL737.M43T47 1995
599.1—dc20

94-24478
CIP
AC

What does it look like?

Where does it live?

What does it eat?

How does it reproduce?

How does it survive?

TURN THESE PAGES AND FIND OUT!

**ADULT ECHIDNAS ARE
COVERED WITH LONG,
SHARP SPINES.**

An echidna is one of the world's weirdest animals. It has a long, thin snout and is covered from head to foot with sharp spines. An echidna is round and prickly and looks something like a porcupine.

chidnas belong to a group of animals called mammals. Scientists have identified about 4,000 kinds, or species, of mammals. There are two species of echidnas. The short-beaked echidna lives in Australia and on the nearby island of New Guinea. The long-beaked echidna lives only on New Guinea.

THE LONG-BEAKED ECHIDNA, WHICH LIVES ON THE ISLAND OF NEW GUINEA, IS ONE OF ONLY TWO SPECIES OF ECHIDNAS.

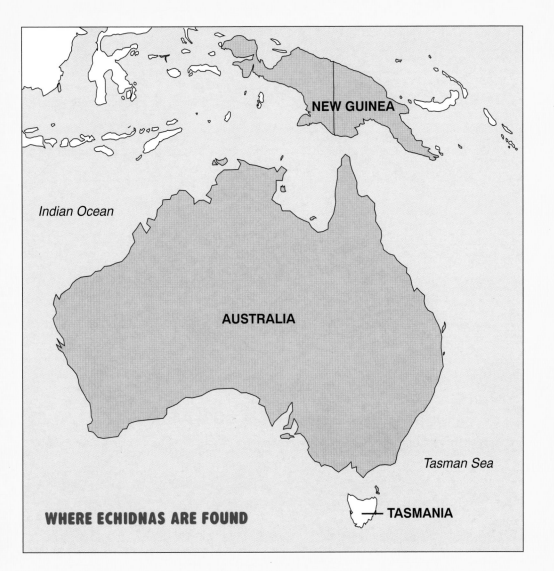

WHERE ECHIDNAS ARE FOUND

Echidnas, like all other mammals, have mammary glands that produce milk. Baby mammals feed on their mother's milk until they are old enough to look for their own food.

Echidnas, unlike other mammals, do not give birth to babies that have developed within the mother's body. Echidnas lay eggs. Besides the two species of echidnas, the platypus is the only mammal that does this. The platypus—which looks like a small beaver with a duck's bill—lives only in Australia.

A SHORT-BEAKED,
ALBINO (ALL WHITE)
ECHIDNA SEARCHES
THE GROUND FOR
FOOD.

Scientists have classified echidnas in the Family Tachyglossidae. The two species of echidnas are the only members of this family. The family name comes from two Greek words meaning "fast tongue." It describes one of the echidna's most important features—its long tongue, which can move very, very quickly when an echidna finds something to eat.

The animal is named after Echidna, a scary monster from an ancient Greek legend. According to this legend, Echidna was killed by a bold young warrior. The warrior filled Echidna's body with arrows—just as the animal today is full of spines.

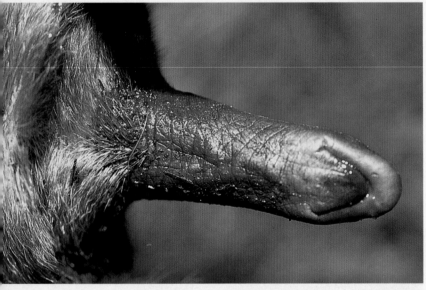

TOP: SHARP SPINES ARE MIXED WITH THE FUR ON AN ECHIDNA'S BACK.
MIDDLE: AN ECHIDNA'S MOUTH IS AT THE END OF A LONG, TUBE-LIKE SNOUT.
BOTTOM: ALL ECHIDNAS HAVE SHARP CLAWS ON THEIR FEET.

The echidna is a plump little creature. When it is fully grown, the echidna is 1 to 2.6 feet (30 to 79 centimeters) long and weighs from 4 to 15 pounds (2 to 7 kilograms). Males and females look alike, but males are bigger than females.

Like most mammals, the echidna's body is covered with fur. Mingled with the fur on the echidna's back are many sharp spines. There are no spines on the animal's belly, legs, or snout.

An echidna's mouth is like a long tube. Inside its mouth is a long, round tongue that looks like a worm. The mouth opens at the tip of the long snout, or beak. The nostrils also open at the tip of the snout. Above the snout are a pair of small, bulging eyes.

The echidna also has a short tail and four short legs. The toes on each foot end in very strong, sharp claws.

Each echidna has its own territory, or area in which it lives. But it doesn't have one specific home within this area. One day it may rest in a hollow log, the next day under a pile of leaves or in a shallow burrow (nest in the ground). As it wanders around its territory, it may even swim across a pond or stream, keeping the tip of its snout above water so it can breathe.

TOP: DURING THE DAY, AN ECHIDNA MIGHT WADE ACROSS A SHALLOW STREAM OR SPEND TIME IN A BURROW (BOTTOM).

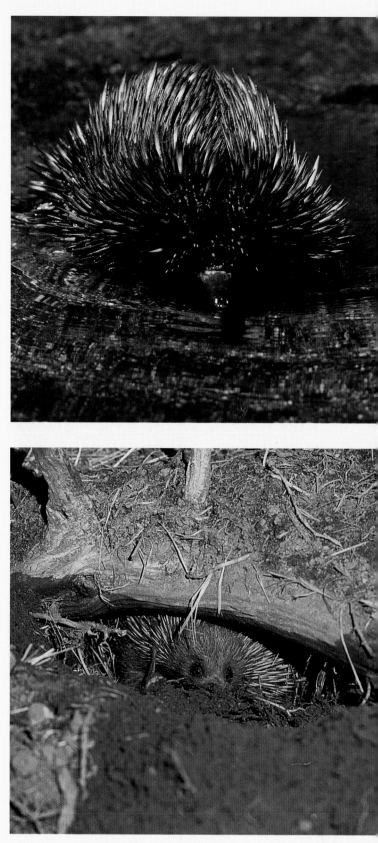

Short-beaked echidnas live in a variety of habitats, from dry grasslands and rocky hillsides to dark, moist forests. Long-beaked echidnas are seldom seen, for they live in mountain forests that are difficult for people to reach.

Echidnas are usually active early in the morning and at sunset. In hot weather, they will come out only at night. During cold weather, they may be most active during the middle of the day. Even though they may swim or get wet, echidnas do not like rain. An echidna may remain curled up in a burrow or log for days, waiting for rain to stop before it wanders out to look for food.

ECHIDNAS LIVE IN MANY DIFFERENT HABITATS. HERE, A SHORT-BEAKED ECHIDNA MAKES ITS HOME IN THE FOREST.

AN ECHIDNA DINES ON TERMITES. INSECTS ARE A LARGE PART OF AN ECHIDNA'S DIET.

Some people have another name for the echidna. They call it the "spiny anteater." Echidnas are not related to anteaters, but this name gives a clue to the echidna's diet. Short-beaked echidnas eat mainly ants and termites. Long-beaked echidnas also eat ants and termites, but their main food seems to be earthworms.

An echidna usually hunts for food by rooting through leaves and other things on the ground. It also uses its strong claws to tear up ant nests and termite nests. An echidna relies on its excellent sense of smell to locate prey. As soon as an echidna finds something tasty, it shoots out its long, sticky tongue. The victim sticks to the tongue, which quickly snaps back into the mouth.

Echidnas have no teeth. Before their food is swallowed, it is mashed between the tongue and the top of the mouth.

AN ECHIDNA USES ITS SHARP CLAWS TO DIG INTO A TERMITE MOUND.

THE RED KANGAROO AND THE POSSUM (OPPOSITE) ARE TWO KINDS OF MAMMALS THAT SHARE THEIR AUSTRALIAN HABITAT WITH THE ECHIDNA.

Echidnas share their habitats with many other animals. There are lizards, turtles, frogs, and numerous birds—including honey-eaters, kookaburras, lyrebirds, and a colorful assortment of parrots.

Most of the mammals in the echidnas' habitats are marsupials. Marsupials are mammals that raise their young in pouches on their bellies. Echidnas that feed early in the morning may pass well-known marsupials such as kangaroos and wallabies, which also look for food at that time of day. Echidnas that feed at night may pass marsupials known as wombats, bandicoots, and pygmy possums, which also search for food when the sun goes down.

Thanks to their covering of sharp spines, echidnas do not have many natural enemies. Occasionally, however, a dingo will attack an echidna. Dingos are wild dogs found only in Australia. They are fierce hunters. In addition to attacking small animals such as echidnas, dingos attack animals much larger than themselves, including kangaroos.

Baby echidnas are sometimes killed and eaten by long-necked lizards called goannas. These lizards use their tongues as organs of smell, helping them to track down echidnas and other kinds of prey.

A DINGO SEARCHES ITS SURROUNDINGS FOR PREY. DINGOS ARE ONE OF
THE FEW NATURAL ENEMIES OF THE ECHIDNA.

An echidna has several excellent defenses against hungry predators. One of its defenses is camouflage. Camouflage means blending into the surroundings in order to be harder to see. An echidna's coloring blends in well with the ground cover of its habitat. This makes it difficult for enemies to see an echidna.

A second defense for an echidna is to curl into a tight ball. In this position, its sharp spines stick out in all directions, making it look like a big pin-cushion.

An echidna has still another defense. When it senses danger, it quickly digs a hole with its strong claws. It digs straight down into the soil, until

TO PROTECT ITSELF, AN ECHIDNA WILL BURROW INTO THE SOIL OR ROLL INTO A TIGHT BALL. THIS WAY, IT EXPOSES ONLY ITS SHARP SPINES TO ITS ENEMIES.

only its spines remain aboveground. This way most of the echidna's body is protected and an enemy is faced only with sharp spines.

Sometimes an echidna will wedge itself into a rock crevice or among the roots of a tree. Its spines grip the surrounding surfaces so tightly that even a large enemy cannot pull it out.

A MALE AND FEMALE ECHIDNA PREPARE TO MATE.

During most of the year, echidnas avoid one another. The only time they are seen in groups is during mating season. Mating is the first step in reproduction—the process of making babies. Reproduction is one of the most important processes for any living thing. Without successful reproduction, a species will eventually die out.

When a female echidna is ready to mate, she leaves a scent trail. A male echidna then follows this trail until he finds the female. During mating, the male deposits sperm cells inside the female's body. When a sperm cell combines with a female's egg cell, the egg becomes fertilized. A fertilized egg contains all the material needed to produce a baby. The fertilized egg then grows into an embryo. An embryo is a developing organism. As the embryo matures, a soft, white shell surrounds it.

A FEMALE ECHIDNA
COMES OUT OF HER
BURROW.

During the mating season, folds of skin on the female echidna's belly enlarge to form a temporary pouch. When the female is ready to lay an egg, she curls up in such a way that the egg rolls into the pouch. The heat of the female's body then keeps the egg warm.

Each echidna lays only one egg at a time. The egg hatches in its mother's pouch about ten days after it is laid.

KEEP O... ...HILDREN
...ONLY

BABY
ECHIDNA

J.F. DOOLEY B.V.Sc.
VETERINARY SURGEON
105 Isabella Street WINGHAM 2429
(065) 53 4325

KEEP OUT OF REACH OF CHILDREN
FOR ANIMAL USE ONLY

ECHIDNA

inside.

J.F. DOOLEY B.V.Sc.
VETERINARY SURGEON
105 Isabella Street WINGHAM 2429
(065) 53 4325

**A BABY ECHIDNA LOOKS LIKE
ITS PARENTS, BUT HAS NO
FUR OR SPINES.**

newborn echidna has no fur and no spines. It is only half an inch (12 millimeters) long. It feeds on the thick milk produced by its mother's mammary glands. This milk slowly oozes from the mother's pores onto hairs in her pouch.

A baby echidna stays in the pouch for about two months. Then, as the baby's spines begin to develop, the mother takes it out of the pouch and puts it in a hidden den. There, she continues to feed the baby for at least another six months.

By the time a young echidna is one year old, it is ready to live on its own. Echidnas have surprisingly long lives. One echidna raised by humans lived to be about 50 years old.

AFTER A FEW MONTHS, A
YOUNG ECHIDNA HAS SOME
FUR ON ITS BODY.

TODAY, ECHIDNA
HABITATS ARE
THREATENED BY
PEOPLE WHO HARM
THE ENVIRONMENT.

Echidnas are common throughout much of
Australia. They are scarce, however, in areas that
are settled by people. People build fences and
roads, which make it difficult for echidnas to
move freely around their territories and meet
mates. Eventually, some of these people may
wish that they hadn't made the environment so
unfriendly to echidnas. Echidnas help control ant
and termite populations. In places where there
are no echidnas, these insects are often serious
pests to humans.

In New Guinea, people hunt long-beaked
echidnas for food. They have also cut down
many of the forests in which long-beaked
echidnas live. As a result, populations of long-
beaked echidnas have been reduced, and the
species is now in danger of dying out, or
becoming extinct. This would be sad. Echidnas
play an important role in their environment. And,
because they are egg-laying mammals, they are
also very unusual and fascinating creatures.

Glossary

burrow Nest in the ground.

camouflage Blending into the surroundings.

extinct A species that has died out, or no longer exists.

fertilization The joining of a male sex cell, called a sperm, and a female sex cell, called an egg. Fertilization is a part of reproduction.

habitat The area where a living thing has its home.

mammary glands Glands in female mammals that produce milk.

predator An animal that hunts other animals for food.

prey An animal that is hunted for food.

reproduction Making more creatures of the same kind.

species A group of living things that are closely related to one another. Members of a species can reproduce with one another.

territory The area in which an animal lives.

Further Reading

Barrett, Norman. *Kangaroos and Other Marsupials.* New York: Franklin Watts, 1991.

Brooks, F. *Protecting Endangered Species.* Tulsa, OK: EDC Publishing, 1991.

Chinery, Michael. *Grassland Animals.* New York: Random House, 1992.

Confort, Kellie. *A Picture Book of Australian Animals.* Mahwah, NJ: Troll, 1992.

Ganeri, Anita. *Small Mammals.* Chicago: Watts, 1993.

Lambert, David. *The Golden Concise Encyclopedia of Mammals.* New York: Western, 1992.

Parsons, Alexandra. *Amazing Mammals.* New York: Random House, 1990.

The Sierra Club Book of Small Mammals. San Francisco: Sierra, 1993.

Stodart, Eleanor. *Australian Echidna.* Boston: Houghton Mifflin, 1991.

Taylor, David. *Endangered Grassland Animals.* New York: Crabtree Publishing, 1992.

Tesar, Jenny. *Mammals.* Woodbridge, CT: Blackbirch Press, Inc., 1993.

Index